Marcy's Bakery

I Talk You Talk Press

CONTENTS

CHAPTER ONE

Marcy Greene stood outside the bakery. She looked up at the sign. *Marcy's Bakery.*

She felt very happy. *My bakery!* she thought. *I have a bakery!*

A man came out of the post office next to the bakery. He stopped and looked at the sign. Then, he looked at Marcy.

"Are you opening a bakery here?" he asked.

"Yes, I am," said Marcy.

"Great! When are you going to open?"

"Tomorrow morning at 8:00am," said Marcy.

"We need a bakery in this town," said the man. "There was a bakery here for a long time. The owner was Ethel Peterson, but she retired five years ago. She worked in the bakery for over fifty years. She closed the shop when she was eighty."

"Really? So she was still baking at that age? That's awesome!" said Marcy.

"Yes, she was an amazing woman. And she was a very good baker. Her cakes were very popular. So, what are you going to sell?"

"Well, of course, I'm going to sell bread," said Marcy. "But I'm also going to sell my special strawberry and cream cupcakes!"

"Awesome! I'm going to work now. I'll tell everyone in my office and in the neighbourhood. Everyone in the town will be very pleased."

"Thank you," said Marcy. "That's very kind of you."

"See you tomorrow!" said the man.

"Yes, see you tomorrow!" said Marcy.

The people in this town are so friendly, thought Marcy. *I'm glad I moved here.*

Marcy moved to New Willow Town a month before she started the bakery. She worked as a chef in a restaurant in Chicago for a long time. However, she didn't like working in the city. She wanted to live in a quiet place with lots of nature. She also wanted to bake bread and cakes. So, she quit her job, and when she found the empty bakery in New Willow Town, she moved there.

The next day, Marcy woke up at 3:00am and went to the bakery. She started baking very early. The bakery was small, but very clean and bright. It had a shop area and a kitchen. At the front of the shop there was a large glass door. There were also two large windows. In the shop, there was a long glass cake counter, and there were many shelves. Marcy put the bread and pastries on the shelves, and put the cakes behind the counter. At 8:00am, she opened the door.

There were many people waiting.

"Marcy's Bakery is open!" said Marcy.

Everyone cheered and ran into the bakery. There were many factory workers and some town office workers. They bought pastries for breakfast.

Between 9:00am and 11:00am, Marcy made many sandwiches.

Then, from 11:00am to 1:00pm, many people came to the bakery to buy sandwiches and strawberry and cream cupcakes.

"This bakery is great! We needed a bakery here," said a woman. "I think this bakery will be very popular."

Then, she ate a strawberry and cream cupcake.

"Oh, this is wonderful! It's so delicious! I'm going to tell all my friends! I work at the supermarket. I will tell all my customers too!"

"Really? Thank you! You are very kind!" said Marcy.

"You're welcome!" said the woman. "I'm Wendy. Nice to meet you."

"I'm Marcy. Nice to meet you too!" said Marcy. They shook hands.

"Marcy, can I take some photographs of these cakes? I want to put the photos on Facebook and on my blog!"

"Sure! Thanks!" said Marcy.

Wendy took many photos. Marcy was very pleased.

Later that afternoon, many people came to Marcy's bakery to buy strawberry and cream cupcakes. She sold out before 4:00pm.

At 5:00pm Marcy closed the doors. She sat down in the kitchen.

"That was a very busy day!" she said to herself. "I sold out of strawberry and cream cupcakes. I have to make more tomorrow!"

CHAPTER TWO

Marcy's bakery soon became very popular. Everybody in the town loved her strawberry and cream cupcakes.

Marcy made many cupcakes every morning. She put the cupcakes on the kitchen table and she put some in the shop cake counter. Every thirty minutes, she had to go back to the kitchen to get more cakes. The cakes sold very quickly.

About a month later, Marcy was sitting in her bakery, waiting for the bread to bake in the oven. She was reading the local newspaper. She saw a story about a bakery. She was very surprised to see a story about a bakery, so she read it carefully.

In the next town, about five miles away, there was a bakery.

In the newspaper story, the owner of the bakery in the next town said, "I am very worried. I have lost many customers. Now, many of my customers go to the new bakery in New Willow Town. They all go to Marcy's Bakery. People from all the other small towns near New Willow go to Marcy's Bakery too. Everyone wants to eat Marcy's strawberry and cream cupcakes."

Marcy finished reading the story. She felt a little sad. But what could she do? She wasn't doing anything bad. She was just making delicious cakes and bread. She was making the people of New Willow Town happy.

She put the newspaper down and took the bread out of the oven. She soon forgot about the story.

A few days later, an old woman came to the bakery.

"Hello Marcy. I'm Ethel Peterson. I was the owner of this bakery many years ago," she said.

"Oh really?" said Marcy. "It's so nice to meet you, Mrs Peterson."

"Oh, please call me Ethel. It's nice to meet you, too," said Ethel, smiling. "I've heard many great things about your cakes. Everyone says they are delicious."

"Thank you," said Marcy. She picked up a strawberry and cream cupcake. "Here you are, Ethel. This is a present from me."

"Oh thank you!" said Ethel. She ate some of the cake. "Oh, this is wonderful! Really wonderful!" she said. "Oh, and your husband is wonderful, too."

"Pardon? My husband? I don't have a husband. I'm single," said Marcy.

"Your husband, Marcy! I met your husband last week! He came to my house. He is a very nice man. He is so kind!" said Ethel.

Marcy didn't understand.

"But, Ethel, I don't have a…"

A man came into the shop.

"Mother! There you are! I've been looking for you!" said the man. "I was worried about you! I told you to wait in the car while I was in the supermarket!"

He looked at Marcy.

"Hi, I'm George. And this is my mother Ethel. My mother Ethel was the owner of this bakery for many years."

"Yes, we were talking about that," said Marcy. "And she thinks she met my husband, but I'm not married!"

"I'm sorry," said George. "My mother is very old. She has a very bad memory now."

Marcy laughed. "Oh, it's OK!"

George and Ethel left the shop.

"But George, her husband came to our house!" said Ethel.

"Come on mother. Let's go home. It's time for your medicine," said George as he helped his mother into the car.

Marcy watched them and smiled.

George and Ethel went home. Marcy had another very busy day. By 2:00pm, all the cream cakes were sold out.

However, a few weeks later, everything changed.

CHAPTER THREE

It was a rainy day, and Marcy was very busy. A man came into the bakery. He was very angry. He started shouting at Marcy.

He said, "I ate a strawberry and cream cupcake! Look at this! I found this paper in the cream! There was paper in the cupcake! This is terrible!"

Everyone looked at the man. He showed all the customers the small piece of white paper.

"No! Marcy is a very good baker! You made a mistake! Maybe it is your paper," said a woman.

"No! It's not my mistake!" said the man. "I found this in the cupcake! Marcy's cupcakes are very dangerous! You shouldn't buy any!"

"But I didn't put paper in my cupcakes! I'm very careful!" said Marcy.

The man looked at her. "But I found it in the strawberry and cream cupcake!" he said. "I will never come here again!" He walked out of the bakery. Some other customers walked out too.

"Don't listen to him Marcy," said one of the women. "Your cupcakes are delicious!"

"Thank you," said Marcy. She smiled at the woman, but she was very shocked and very worried.

That night, she looked everywhere in her kitchen. There were no pieces of paper in the kitchen.

The man made a mistake, she thought. *The man made a mistake.*

The next day, the same woman came into the shop. She looked very upset.

"Marcy, I have to tell you something," she said quietly. "I ate one of your strawberry and cream cupcakes yesterday, and then...I...I found this paper in the cream."

The woman showed Marcy a small piece of paper.

"What? No! No! There is no paper in my kitchen!" said Marcy. "And I'm a very careful baker!" She was very shocked. What was happening?

"I'm sorry Marcy. I believe you. I really do...but...I promise you...I found it in your cupcake," said the woman.

Then, another woman came in.

"Look at this! Look at this!" she said. "I found a piece of paper in my cupcake! Give me my money back! I'm going to tell the government health department!"

Marcy wanted to cry. This was terrible! Why was this happening? Her cupcakes were so popular! And she was always so careful in the kitchen. She cleaned it very carefully every night, and there were no other workers at the bakery. She couldn't understand it.

The women left the shop, and Marcy sat down behind the counter. The bakery was empty. After that, no-one came to buy cupcakes or bread.

A few hours later, a man wearing a suit came to Marcy's bakery.

He said, "Are you Marcy Greene?"

"Yes, I am," said Marcy.

"I am an inspector from the government health department. Today, many people called us. They said, 'We found pieces of paper in Marcy's cupcakes'. So, we are going to check your bakery. You have to close for a week while we check everything."

Marcy looked at the man. She was very shocked.

"But there is no paper in my kitchen! I'm a very careful baker! I don't understand! You have made a mistake!"

"You have to close the shop. Give me the key," said the man.

"No!" said Marcy. "I work so hard! I'm very careful!"

"Give me the key!" said the man loudly.

The man looked very angry. Marcy gave him the key.

"Please go home," said the man. "We will call you next week."

Marcy walked out of the bakery very slowly. The man closed the door. He turned the sign on the door from "open" to "closed".

Marcy went home to her apartment near the lake. She sat on the balcony and watched the sunset. She thought about her life. She worked very hard in the bakery. Everyone liked her cupcakes. Her bakery was very popular. But now, her life was like a nightmare.

Why did people find pieces of paper in the cakes? Why? she thought. *It's very strange. What am I going to do?*

That night, she couldn't sleep. She was worrying about her cupcakes and her customers.

Marcy spent the next week alone in her apartment. When she went out, people looked at her and pointed at her.

"There is Marcy, the bad baker!" they said to each other.

Marcy didn't want to go out anymore. She spent most of the time at home, looking at the lake or watching TV.

CHAPTER FOUR

A week later, the government inspector called Marcy.

"Ms Greene, we have checked your bakery. We didn't find anything strange. You can re-open tomorrow."

"Thank you! Thank you!" said Marcy. She was very happy.

She went to the supermarket and bought some eggs, sugar and milk.

"You are buying many eggs and a lot of milk, Marcy. Are you going to open your bakery again?" asked Wendy, the supermarket cashier. Marcy liked Wendy. She was always very friendly and kind to Marcy.

"Yes, I am! The government inspector didn't find any problems!" said Marcy.

"Oh good! I'm very glad!" said Wendy. "I will come to your shop to buy some cupcakes tomorrow!"

"Thank you Wendy!" said Marcy. "I'm going to have a half-price sale tomorrow. All pastries and cupcakes are half-price!"

"Great! I will tell my friends on Facebook and Twitter!" said Wendy.

The next day, Marcy went to the bakery at 4:00am. She baked the bread and made the cupcakes. She put the cupcakes on the table in the kitchen, and put some of them on the shop counter. Then, she opened the bakery at 8:00am.

Wendy and her friends came to the shop. They bought many strawberry and cream cupcakes because they were half-price. Many people came to the bakery again. Marcy was very happy.

At 2:00pm, Wendy came back to the bakery. She looked upset.

"Hi again, Wendy. Do you want some more cakes?" said Marcy.

"Marcy, look!" said Wendy. She showed Marcy a small piece of plastic. "I found this in the cupcake."

Marcy looked at Wendy and then at the small piece of white plastic in Wendy's hand. "What? What? I don't believe it!" said Marcy.

"I'm sorry Marcy. It's true," said Wendy. "And my friend found a small piece of plastic, too."

Marcy sat down. "I don't understand. I didn't put the plastic in the cupcake. I didn't," said Marcy.

"I believe you Marcy," said Wendy. "But, if you didn't put the plastic in the cupcakes…who did?"

Marcy and Wendy looked at each other. Then, Marcy had an idea.

"Wendy, are you free tomorrow lunch time?" asked Marcy.

"Yes, I am. Why?"

"Can you work in the bakery tomorrow lunch time?"

"Yes, of course," said Wendy. "What are you going to do?"

"I'm going to watch my cakes in the kitchen," said Marcy.

CHAPTER FIVE

The next day, Marcy made the cupcakes and pastries and put them on the table in the kitchen. At lunchtime, Wendy came to the bakery and worked in the shop.

In the kitchen, there was a big box. Marcy cut two small holes in the box. Then, she got into the box and closed the lid. She looked through the holes in the box. She could see most of the kitchen and the refrigerator area. She stayed in the box for a long time. Nothing happened.

This is a bad idea, she thought. *No one is here. There is no one here.* She started to get out of the box. Then, she heard a sound. She stopped and looked at the back door. It sounded like a key.

She got back in the box and put the lid down. Then, she heard the door open.

Someone is here! she thought.

Through the holes in the box Marcy saw a man walk into the kitchen. Very quietly, he took some pieces of plastic out of his bag. Then, he put them in the cupcakes on the table.

Marcy was shocked. *What is he doing?* she thought. Then, she felt angry. Very angry.

Why is this man here, in MY kitchen? He is putting plastic in MY cakes!

She stood up and shouted, "Why are you here in my kitchen?"

The man was very shocked. He tried to run out of the kitchen, but Marcy grabbed him. She pushed him against the wall. He fell onto the floor.

"What are you doing?" she shouted.

Marcy picked the man up off the floor and pushed him against the refrigerator.

Wendy came into the kitchen.

"Marcy? Are you OK?" she said. Then, she saw the man.

"What's happening? Who is he?" she shouted.

"This man put plastic in my cupcakes!" said Marcy.

"What?!" said Wendy. "Let's call the police!"

Marcy looked at the man.

"Yes! Call the police! Quick!" said Marcy.

"I'm sorry! I'm sorry! Don't call the police! Please! I'm sorry!" said the man.

Marcy looked at him. He was around twenty-two years old, and he looked very frightened.

"It's you! You put pieces of paper and plastic in my cupcakes!" she shouted. "Why? Why?"

"I'm sorry! I'm sorry!" said the man. "Please! Don't hurt me!"

Marcy pushed him onto a chair.

"Sit there and explain!" she shouted. The man put his head in his hands.

"My mother and father are the owners of the bakery in the next town. They had a good business. Everyone loved their cakes. Then, you opened your bakery. All of our customers started going to your bakery because your strawberry and cream cupcakes are delicious. They are better than my family's cakes. My family makes very good sandwiches but people won't go to one bakery for cakes and another bakery for sandwiches. So, our bakery is in trouble. My mother and father spent all their lives building that bakery. Then, you opened your bakery and…" The man looked very sad. He shook his head. "And…they lost many customers."

"So, you started to come here and put pieces of paper and plastic in my cupcakes?" asked Marcy.

The man looked at the floor. He couldn't look at Marcy.

"Yes," he said quietly.

"Do your mother and father know about this?" asked Marcy. "Do they know about the pieces of paper and the plastic? Do they know you are a very bad son?"

The man shook his head. "No, they don't," he said quietly.

"We are going to see your mother and father now," said Marcy. She put her coat on.

"Wendy, can you stay here for another hour?" asked Marcy.

"Sure. I start work at the supermarket at 3:00pm, so I can stay until 2:30pm," said Wendy.

"Thanks," said Marcy. She pushed the man out of the door and into her car.

CHAPTER SIX

They drove to the man's family bakery in the next town. They went into the bakery. The bakery was small, and there were no customers at all.

The man's mother and father were in the shop. They were around sixty years old and looked very gentle and kind.

"Good afternoon. Can I help you?" said the man's mother to Marcy.

"Your son has something to tell you," said Marcy.

The man's mother and father looked surprised.

"What is it?" said the man's father.

In the bakery, the man told his parents about the pieces of paper and the plastic.

"Jerry! Why did you do that? You stupid boy!" said the man's father. He was very angry.

"I wanted to help you!" said Jerry. "When Marcy's Bakery opened, many of our customers stopped coming here. They all went to Marcy's Bakery because her strawberry and cream cupcakes are delicious. We lost a lot of money."

His mother looked at him. "Yes, we lost a lot of money. But your actions were very bad!"

Jerry's father looked at Marcy. "What are you going to do Ms Greene?" he asked.

"I don't know," said Marcy.

Everyone stopped talking. They were thinking about the terrible situation.

"I think you have to tell the police," said Jerry's father. "Of course, I don't want my son to be in trouble with the police. But he has done a very bad thing. He must be punished."

"Yes, I have to tell the police," said Marcy.

"But, I don't want other people to hear about this. If people hear about this, no one will ever come to our bakery. My wife and I spent many years building this bakery," said Jerry's father.

"It's OK. I will only tell the police. I won't tell anyone else. But, what about my bakery? My customers? Everyone thinks I put pieces of paper and plastic in my cupcakes. No one will come to my bakery anymore."

Jerry's father thought for a minute. Then he said, "How about I write a letter to the newspaper? I will write 'Someone entered Ms Greene's bakery and put pieces of paper and plastic in the cupcakes. I am very shocked. I am a baker too. I understand how hard Ms Greene works in her bakery. She is a professional baker and her cupcakes are delicious. Ms Greene is innocent.' What do you think Marcy? Will that be okay for you?"

Marcy thought about it. It was a good idea. "Yes, that will be fine. Thank you," she said.

Marcy felt bad because Jerry's mother and father lost customers. They were very nice people. She didn't want their bakery to lose money. She thought for a few minutes. Then, she had an idea.

"Would you like to sell my cupcakes, too?" asked Marcy. "I can bake them and you can arrange to collect them every day. Then, people will come to your bakery too. I know you make great sandwiches and if people come to buy cupcakes, they will buy sandwiches too."

Jerry's mother and father looked at each other. Then, they looked at Marcy. They smiled.

"That's a great idea!" said Jerry's mother. "Yes! Thank you!"

"Great! I'll make extra cakes tomorrow morning!" said Marcy. She looked at Jerry.

"Why did you have a key to my bakery?" she asked Jerry.

Jerry looked at the floor. He didn't say anything.

"Why did you have a key?" shouted Jerry's father. "Answer the question!"

"Well…I saw Mrs Peterson, the old baker, in the post office. She is very old now. I said, 'I am Marcy Greene's husband. Do you have an extra key for the back door of the bakery?' She said, 'Oh yes, I have a back door key in my house. Come with me. I will give you the key.' So, I went to her house and she gave me the key," said Jerry.

Jerry's mother, father and Marcy looked at him. They were very shocked.

"I am ashamed of you!" said his father. "You are not my son anymore!"

"I'm sorry," said Jerry.

"Get out!" shouted his mother. "Get out of here!"

"I'm sorry Ms Greene. I really am sorry," he said quietly.

"We are so sorry Ms Greene," said his mother.

"But don't worry," said his father. "We will tell the newspaper. Everything will be fine."

"Thank you," said Marcy. "OK Jerry. Get in the car. We are going to the police station."

Marcy took Jerry to the police station. The police gave Jerry a severe warning.

Then, Marcy went to the hardware store and bought a new lock and keys for her bakery.

CHAPTER SEVEN

Jerry's father wrote to the newspaper. The newspaper put the story about the bakery on the front page. Many people saw the story and came to Marcy's shop.

Some people asked, "Who was the man, Marcy?"

But Marcy didn't tell anyone Jerry's name. She didn't want his mother and father to have more trouble.

Marcy's bakery became very popular again, and many customers came to buy cupcakes.

Everyday Jerry's mother and father sold Marcy's strawberry and cream cupcakes in their bakery. Their bakery also became very popular again.

Marcy's bakery was very busy, so she needed some help. Wendy quit her job at the supermarket and started working at the bakery. Marcy and Wendy became very good friends and now they enjoy working together. Jerry's mother and father forgave their son. Jerry started working at his mother and father's bakery again. Now, he works very hard to sell Marcy's strawberry and cream cupcakes.

The supermarket in New Willow Town also started to sell Marcy's strawberry and cream cupcakes. After a year, a large national supermarket started to sell them too. Now, Marcy has a factory and five stores in the Chicago area. Everyone loves Marcy's cupcakes, and Marcy loves her job and her life in New Willow Town.

THANK YOU

Thank you for reading Marcy's Bakery! We hope you enjoyed Marcy's story. (Word count: 3,973)

There are quizzes about this book on our free study site I Talk You Talk Press EXTRA. http://italk-youtalk.com

If you would like to read more graded readers, please visit our website
http://www.italkyoutalk.com

Other Level 2 graded readers include
Adventure in Rome
Andre's Dream
A Passion for Music
Christmas Tales
Danger in Seattle
Don't Come Back
Finders Keepers…
Men's Konkatsu Tales
Salaryman Secrets!
Stories for Halloween
The Perfect Wedding
The House in the Forest
The School on Bolt Street
Train Travel

Trouble in Paris
Women's Konkatsu Tales

ABOUT THE AUTHOR

I Talk You Talk Press is a Japan-based publisher of language textbooks, graded readers and language learning/teaching resources.

Our team is made up of highly experienced language teachers and translators, who have all studied at least one additional language to an advanced level.

This experience enables us to design our materials from the perspective of both the teacher and the learner. We consult with both teachers and language learners when designing our textbooks and graded readers, and test our materials extensively in the classroom before publication.

We are a fast-growing press, and currently publish graded readers for learners of English. We publish new graded readers monthly.

Marcy's Bakery

I Talk You Talk Press

www.ingramcontent.com/pod-product-compliance
Lightning Source LLC
Chambersburg PA
CBHW022352040426
42449CB00006B/845